D0946304

THE *Beckoning* RIDE

IZZIE STRAWN

This book is a work of non-fiction. Unless otherwise noted, the author and the publisher make no explicit guarantees as to the accuracy of the information contained in this book and in some cases, names of people and places have been altered to protect their privacy.

WestBow Press books may be ordered through booksellers or by contacting:

WestBow Press
A Division of Thomas Nelson & Zondervan
1663 Liberty Drive
Bloomington, IN 47403
www.westbowpress.com
844-714-3454

ISBN: 978-1-6642-5864-8 (sc)
ISBN: 978-1-6642-5866-2 (hc)
ISBN: 978-1-6642-5865-5 (e)

Library of Congress Control Number: 2022903377

Print information available on the last page.

WestBow Press rev. date: 03/22/2022

Contents

Preface

My experience happened before the COVID-19 locked out visitors in nursing homes. Visitors were free to come and go into the facility. I had always felt a flash of danger when I navigated the halls. I felt as if I was entering the mouth of a doomed, dark cave. I reminded myself that most of the residents were helpless and had no one to watch out for them. Emptiness lurked in every corner.

The perilous journey my brother and I took while he was in the nursing home resembled traveling on foot through the desert. We had plenty of food and water. Rescue was impossible. We had no map or compass for directions. No one seemed to notice.

I'd been told I was to be the hero of my story. But looking back, I think perhaps my brother was the real hero. He endured illnesses, a broken health-care system, hostile nursing homes, abandonment, deceit, and eventually death. He never complained. We strived to keep him alive and comfortable.

Who was the real hero in this story?

You can decide as you read.

Chapter 1

RUN LIKE THE WIND

I GRIPPED THE PHONE TIGHTER AS I HEARD MY SISTER'S VOICE. "Come as quick as you can," she shouted. "It's Cal. He wouldn't answer his phone."

Her words came in a rush. "I called the fire department to go to his house. They had to take off the back door. Found him on the floor by his bed. They took him to the hospital. Hurry!"

And then she hung up.

"Wait, wait."

That was all.

Cal. My brother. My hero.

A voice inside me screamed, *Go!*

I grabbed my fleece. My shaggy, uncombed hair bounced; my fuzzy house shoes flopped on my feet. I grabbed my keys from the kitchen counter and tossed my coffee into the sink.

No time for makeup, but I had on clean clothes.

The cold wind hurled sand and dirt as I drove my car from Dallas. *Steady. Stay calm*. My mind raced. What had happened? Would I lose my brother? Would he ever get to leave the hospital? For seventy-five miles, I drove, clinging to the steering wheel as if on a racetrack.

I spotted the small, red brick hospital. I aimed my car into a tight parking spot. The car bumped the curb, and I rocked back and forth, a ship on a stormy sea.

A wave of antiseptic smell overwhelmed me as I stepped inside the old building. The glossy tile floor looked wet.

Right away, a young receptionist called to me. "You must be here to see Cal?"

Word certainly got around here. I rushed to the room she pointed to, trying to harness my fears. My sister must have heard me. She stepped out and motioned for me to come in. I took a deep breath before I entered the room.

"Someone hurt him, I think," she said.

I dropped my purse by a chair and rushed to his bed. My heart sank. His eyes, deep blue, looked weary. His gray hair was askew. His six-foot frame overpowered the small, old-fashioned hospital bed.

I touched his weathered arm. How did he get so old? "Cal, it's Izzie. I'm here."

He looked away when I asked what happened, remained silent, and stared out the window.

I remembered he'd been robbed before. He hadn't wanted to talk that time either.

I turned to my sister. "What happened?"

"I think someone came back for money, and he refused to give it to them," she said.

I looked at my brother. "Cal?"

Was he afraid he could be in danger if he revealed who did this to him?

A middle-aged doctor rushed into the room. His ostrich boots and western jeans showed below his white coat. The heavy thudding of his boots matched my heartbeat.

"Here's the situation," he said. "There are no broken bones or a head injury. However, he is badly bruised and can't walk. His COPD seems to be under control. His blood pressure is extremely high. Some bodily functions have stopped working. He's not very responsive. He can't go back home by himself for a long time."

I sank into a chair. How could this be? Cal had been like a father to me. He'd cooked, cleaned, and walked me to school. I'd followed him everywhere.

Was it now my turn to take care of him?

My future was uncertain. I had just retired and had been looking forward to a well-earned rest. I had more questions than answers. I was devastated.

Was I capable of helping someone so ill?

I pushed the doubts away. He was my brother, and I would fight for his recovery.

Chapter 2

SNOW DAY

I STARED OUT MY WINDOW AT THE FALLING SNOW. THE PHONE rang. My heart started racing. Cal had been in the hospital only three days. Was this call about him? Was he alright?

"Come and get your brother. Medicare will not pay for him to stay any longer," the doctor said.

What did the doctor mean?

I had left Cal at the hospital yesterday. Overnight, the snow had piled higher, and icicles dangled from my roof. I had been stranded at home, two hours away from the hospital, the mountain road barricaded.

"I can't get there," I said. "Can't he stay until the roads are clear and I can get there?"

"No, he can't stay," he said.

What did that doctor expect me to do, rent a snowplow?

I descended into a whirlpool of hopelessness. Why are our elderly treated like delicate flowers tossed by an ungrateful wind?

"He has to stay," I said. "Is he even well enough to be moved in this weather?"

"Doesn't matter. Insurance does. Come get him," the doctor said.

Did this guy expect miracles? I imagined the doctor having Cal pushed out in the lobby and left there, alone, sick, and afraid. I blocked my tears, hung up the phone, and tried to think rationally.

I couldn't forgive myself for leaving him there last night. I'd thought he would be safe. I felt isolated and helpless. I started cleaning the kitchen counter, aching for a solution. The ringing startled me. Now what? Filled with desperation, I managed a hello. Cal's nurse must have overheard the doctor's conversation with me.

"I'm sorry you were put in this position. There is a small nursing home ten minutes from the hospital. It's old, but they take good care of their patients. I know the nurses there. Call this number and see if they have a place for him. I know they have a transport for their patients. I will take care of the paperwork," she said.

Her compassion surprised me.

My spirits lifted for Cal. I jotted down the number and thanked her. The van would come the short distance through the snow and ice. Who were they? Would the facility be warm enough? Would Cal know some of the patients there? I had taken a risky chance.

Cal liked to go—just anywhere. I joked with him about being the first one in my car and that he would ride until I ran out of gas. He always wanted to stop for a cup of coffee.

I imagined Cal's conversation with the nurse. I'm sure she told him about people she knew there. He would beam and be ready to go. He would ask for coffee. She would help him get dressed. Darkness would be creeping in when they went out into the bitter snow to the van.

She phoned back. My tears subsided.

"Two aides and I loaded him very carefully into the van, and he was taken to the nursing home facility. He's going to be fine until you get there," she said.

My fears melted. He would be safe. I had no idea what the nursing home looked like, but the nurse had known.

I trusted her.

I knew the town would be snowed in for at least a week. I waited for the thaw.

Texas weather soon showed its unpredictable self. The sun blazed, and a thaw came. Spring weather emerged out of the snow. I drove to the nursing home only to find another red brick building. Brown grass slept in the sidewalk cracks. Green buds rested on the tall, skinny oak branches along the front. Puddles of melted snow appeared like mirrors on the brown lawn. What was inside? I became leery. My anxiety grew. I pulled open the heavy glass door and entered, stepping on polished, original wood floors. A savory aroma of something cooking filled the lobby. Newspapers cluttered the threadbare vintage sofa. The tattered beige rug could have passed for a fashionable, well-worn antique Persian carpet. A Western movie blared on the old, heavy, black television. No one was watching. The claw-footed game table had scratches and held a well-worn chess set. Had I stepped into a time warp? Where was everyone?

The side room contained a barber chair and a long mirror on the wall. No one there. Not upscale, I thought, but essential. I entered on the polished tile floors, stepping toward the nurses' station. I tried to convince myself the medical staff was qualified. An aide approached me.

"You must be Cal's sister. I heard you were coming. He is adjusting well," the aide said.

Word gets around even in here, I thought.

His tiny room wasn't what I'd expected. Clean bedding and polished floors. Gray, heavy curtains darkened the room. He nestled in his wheelchair, clean and dressed in his jeans and blue shirt, watching the news. He recognized me. Cal could have spent every moment in self-pity, but he always smiled when he saw someone. He would grin when you brought him something special to eat.

He told me he'd gone shopping and out to eat. His comment was a little off. Not like Cal.

"What did you buy?" I asked.

He ignored my question. I wondered if there were more issues than we thought.

"Can I have some more chewing tobacco?" he asked.

This was a good sign, I told myself. He loved his chewing tobacco.

"I'll find out from the nurse if we can go get you some," I said.

I slipped out to the nurses' station. A young nurse smiled as she looked up from her immense stack of patient charts. Would she ignore my request?

"Good morning. I'm Cal's sister. Is he allowed to go out for a ride?" I asked.

Her dark brown eyes looked up, and she pleasantly acknowledged my presence. "Of course, but I do detect something is not quite right with him," she said.

She lifted the old black phone and called an aide to put him the car.

"I detect a problem too. I will keep him safe," I said.

The aide resembled a professional weightlifter. He wheeled Cal efficiently out the door. I scurried after them and unlocked the car. A medication nurse came running out behind us with pills and a cup of water. The aide lifted Cal out of his wheelchair like a feather pillow and set him down in the car seat. Cal swallowed the numerous pills with a gulp of water, handed the cup back, and waved goodbye. They watched us leave.

I stopped for tobacco and asked him if he would mind waiting for me in the car. I had found a parking spot in front of the convenience store. I knew I couldn't get him out by myself. He waved his hand in acknowledgment. I rolled down the windows, hoping he would enjoy the fresh spring air. Watching him from the store window, I quickly scanned the tobacco shelf. There was Red Man tobacco, Copenhagen, and Skoal. His favorite, Beechnut tobacco in a pouch, wasn't there. There were others in a pouch. I picked up a Red Man pouch thinking Babe Ruth and Levi Garrett had perhaps chewed that brand. I hoped Cal would too. I checked out and hurriedly rushed back to the car.

I handed him the pouch of Red Man. He took it, smiled, and laid it in his lap.

"Cup of coffee from Sonic," Cal said.

I had been waiting for those words. I had come to love the way Cal wanted his dark black coffee, the same way my dad and grandad did. Their coffee was brewed rich and thick. I wondered if a spoon could stand up in the dark black liquid. The aroma always created an air of happiness, magic, and well-being for me. I had almost let those cherished memories slip away.

"Sonic it is," I said.

His blue eyes drooped as we drove through Sonic. I parked the car, rolled the windows down, and waited for our coffee. I relished the cool breeze.

My heart skipped a beat. A wasp whizzed in the window and hovered over our heads.

Cal sat still and glanced at me.

"Leave it alone. It'll leave in a minute," he said.

He sat leisurely.

I panicked, unable to move. I struggled to keep calm. What would I do if the pest didn't leave? Should I swat it? My cell phone started ringing in my purse. My fear rose with every ring. I didn't dare move. The wasp landed on the dashboard and hesitated. My heart had been racing with fear as I watched the wasp flapping its velvety wings. In an instant, the unwanted insect dashed over my head and out the window. I frantically closed the windows; glad the wasp's stopover was terminated.

Cal smiled.

I smiled back, now desperate for coffee.

The sweet smell of our coffee uplifted me. We continued our ride to his house. He didn't want to get out in the driveway. I wondered if he was afraid of what had happened the last time he'd been there. I wish I knew. I decided not to ask questions and backed out of the driveway. He continued the ride undisturbed, sipping his coffee.

My heart sank as I pulled into the old, unwished-for building. I had to leave him there. I didn't have a choice. The weightlifter came to the car and took him inside.

For weeks, he spent all his time in the wheelchair. He never complained. His progress went rock bottom. We had to search in the city and find a newer nursing home.

Chapter 3

BABY FLASHBACK

CAL CHOKED DOWN THE TASTELESS NURSING HOME dinner. He asked to go back to his small room. His clothing bulged from the incredibly small, cramped closet. A heavy beige curtain separated his part of the room from that of his roommate. Out the window, a hint of sunset appeared in the distance. Cal twisted in the wheelchair and pointed to the stack of diapers.

"I can't believe all those diapers are mine. I changed your diapers when you were a baby, and now it's my turn for diapers."

"Can you tell me about when I was a baby?" I asked. "I'll listen as long as you want me to."

He hadn't talked much, but he nodded yes. Anxious

to hear, I sat in the threadbare chair beside him. I strained to hear his voice, which was almost a whisper.

"Mama yelled at me all the time after you were born," he said. "'Take care of your crying sister,' she would say."

"All the time?" I asked.

His eyes shifted to the scuffed tile floor as he told me how tired Mama had been.

He remembered how he always scrubbed at the sink full of dirty dishes. Cal said he told her he had been washing dishes and already helped her with the first baby. Why did he have to help with another? I told her I wanted to go outside. Mama told me she couldn't take care of this baby by herself.

"So, I finally gave in and left the dishes to soak," he said. "I shook the suds off my hands."

"Wait a minute," I said. "How did you feel about that. Do you hate me?""

Cal frowned. "I was disappointed, that's all."

I took a deep breath, trying to push down the incredible sadness I felt.

Cal fidgeted in the wheelchair and lifted himself to one side to get comfortable. He continued.

I anxiously listened.

"I tiptoed into the dark room. Two cribs. Baby Sis had her leg over the railing of the crib trying to climb out." He said he demanded she get back in there. "You were wailing. I rushed over to your crib. Now I had to change diapers," he said.

I gasped. "You had to change diapers too?" I asked.

Cal was not yet ten.

He said Mama had showed him how to rinse the cloth diaper and put it in the big pail.

Cal hesitated and caught his breath. "Out of the corner of my eye, I caught some movement in the room. I knew exactly what was happening. Baby Sis was always toddling around the room. I couldn't chase her," he said.

"Two babies for you to watch," I said.

He nodded and graciously continued. "Mama said she needed her cough medicine, but I told her she'd taken the last of it."

"Oh no," I said and moved closer to him.

He was immersed in the story now. He said he left me crying in the crib and put his arms around baby sis's waist and heaved her back over into the crib.

My heart sank as I imagined my brother in such an impossible situation.

After a moment of silence, Cal blurted out, "Mama appeared in the door. Her hair was sticking out everywhere, nightgown and robe all tattered and wrinkled. She wanted her medicine. She told me to watch the babies."

Mama and her medicine. I shivered. I moved closer to the edge of my chair. The room seemed to be getting colder now. I grabbed the blanket at the foot of Cal's bed and put it over his lap.

"What did she do?" I asked.

Cal seemed to be reliving the moment. "Mama snatched her long coat and well-worn shoes out of the closet. The winter day was dreary. She said she hoped her prescription was still good and that she could drive without help."

"Hold on, Cal," I said. "She'd taken that medicine for as long as I can remember. She must have been desperate."

Cal's eyes met mine.

The sky grew darker outside. I turned on the bedside lamp as Cal yawned.

I imagined Mama with her car keys in her hand, slamming the door behind her, Cal alone in the house in the dark baby room, stretching out on the floor when the old Ford pulled away.

Cal now gazed into nothingness in the stillness of the tiny room. Holding back my tears, I leaned over to give him a hug. His body was tense.

"Oh, Cal. I'm so sorry."

He didn't answer.

There was only silence.

Chapter 4

MEDICINE JUNGLE

CAL'S HEAD DROOPED. I NUDGED HIS SHOULDER AND straightened him in the wheelchair. No response.

Was he in a coma? Had someone given him sleeping pills?

I swallowed hard. Fear gripped me when I struggled to move his chair out the door toward the front. I knew the call lights took too long to get help. I approached the nurses' station. The staff had tagged me as a troublemaker. *Stay calm,* I thought. Juanita was almost hidden behind the stack of reports for her seventy-five patients.

"Good morning," I said.

"Yes?" she said.

"I can't wake him up," I said.

Juanita removed her glasses; she looked at me and then at Cal. She rolled her chair back, gazing at the overwhelming stack of reports. I wondered how many hours she'd worked last night. She straightened Cal in the wheelchair. He slid back and didn't open his eyes. She connected the blood pressure gauge. Her eyes widened. She gripped the cell phone in her pocket.

She rapidly spilled out words I couldn't hear.

I moved closer to her.

She ended the call and stared at me.

"His blood pressure is 30/60. I called the ambulance," she said.

She's scared. I'm terrified. I panicked, grabbed the wheelchair handles, and started pushing Cal toward the front door.

"Bring me the necessary papers while I wait out front," I said.

I stood with Cal under the front awning. The hot air flowed through, engulfing us. Beads of sweat rolled down my face. My hair hung limp and lifeless. Cal sat hovered on the edge of darkness.

"Hang on, Cal," I said.

The sound of the ambulance siren stirred my fear.

Paramedics exited, whisked Cal up on their gurney, and slid him inside. The double doors snapped shut. I could only stand and stare. My legs felt like melting wax. I stumbled toward my car. The ambulance didn't move. I hesitated, questioning the wait. No movement. I went back and circled the ambulance. No driver. I felt like Jaws wanting to get in the boat. I couldn't wait any longer. I rapped on the ambulance back door and raised my voice.

"I'm Cal's sister. What's happening?" I asked.

The door creaked opened. A uniformed, young paramedic emerged. There wasn't a flaw in his smooth black hair. His big muscles and gentle manner enhanced his smile. He looked down as I stood helpless on the hot concrete.

"He's OK. We only needed to do something," he said.

My heartbeat slowed. I thanked him and retreated to my car. I dropped steadily in the seat, whirling my tote in the back seat. The contents scattered. I didn't care. I collapsed my head on the steering wheel.

"At least he's still alive," I whispered.

I felt overwhelmed and lonely as the whine of the ambulance took him away.

I had returned to the "bottomless pit" of emergency rooms. I longed for the smell of fresh ground coffee. I wanted a delicious lunch. If only Cal could have sat with me and told me about his memories from the past, memories no one else would have known. I wanted to know how he'd lived without a cell phone or a computer? Why had he loved his chewing tobacco?

The nurse called my name. I jumped up, startled and scared. She handed me a list of Cal's nursing home medications.

"How is Cal?" I asked.

"He's being taken care of. Please verify this list for me. You are the next of kin," she said.

That wasn't a good answer, I thought.

I knew the medication list well. No problem.

Wrong again.

"I recognize all the medications but one," I said. "What is this one?"

The nurse looked up puzzled.

"That's for seizures. Why?" she asked.

"My brother has never had a seizure in his life or this medicine. Call the nursing home," I said.

She frowned and grabbed the phone.

"They said that they have to get back with me," she said.

The thought occurred to me that maybe this medication had brought him down.

"Hang in there, Cal," I whispered.

I gazed at the nurse.

"Since I'm the next of kin, I have the authority to tell you to take this medication off his list," I said.

The nurse smiled. I'm sure she had been through this before.

That night seemed like an endless desert walk. I tossed and turned in my bed. No dreams, just anger, a feeling of betrayal and burning hopelessness.

A surge of strength took me to the nursing home the next morning. I demanded to see Cal's medication list. The supervisor went through her files and handed the papers toward me. "Look it over," she said.

She stared at me as I scoured the list.

"You had a medication on the list yesterday and sent the list to the hospital. Where's that list with the medication?" I asked.

She folded her arms. "This is the only list we ever had," she said.

I gave her back the list and walked away. I thought about saying thank you, but anger kept me moving. I spotted the medicine cart. Carla had been giving patients their morning meds. I peered over her shoulder, trying to read labels on the bottles.

"What medicine are you giving Cal today?" I asked.

She frowned.

"Is that particular medicine I see on your cart for Cal?" I asked.

She stared at the floor and hesitated.

"That's for Cal's roommate," she said.

Chapter 5
ROADSIDE AWARENESS

Another beautiful Texas sunrise glowed as I drove through a gust of leaves being scattered by the wind. I reached for the dial of my radio. This time every Sunday, I listened to my favorite broadcast when I drove to the nursing home. The priest had a sermon that seemed to fit just what I needed. His words helped me make my time at the nursing home less turbulent. I had been overwhelmed observing the illnesses, the pain when someone died, and the tossing away of our precious elderly.

The choir sang. The priest began.

"The sermon today is about the valuable lessons of giving up on your situation," he said.

Did he say I could give up?

"One of the lessons is that you can't justify giving up," he said.

What was he talking about? I was confused. I almost ran off the road.

I kept control of the car, pulled off the road, and parked. I fumbled for a pen in my big tote but only found my lip pencil. That had to do, I must remember this. I slid the napkin from under my coffee cup and started jotting notes on it. Trucks whizzed by me, jolting my car like one small earthquake after another.

"God's sustaining grace may not change the situation but will give you strength to get through it. God doesn't promise an explanation," he said.

Well now, that could really make sense. When I didn't get explanations, I felt frustrated and alone.

I stared out the window at the rolling hills dotted with cactus and scrawny mesquite trees.

He proceeded.

"God ignites a spark within us to go on—a new surge of determination. His grace is there for you when everyone else walks away. There is always a lesson to learn," he said.

Oh no. I didn't want to learn another lesson right now. Breast cancer, divorce, raising three children, and bankruptcy had been all the lessons I needed to know for a lifetime. I should have been the most knowledgeable person alive—but no. I realized there had been more lessons for me to learn about death, my brother, God, and not giving up.

I folded the napkin on the seat and observed my used-up lip pencil. The priest wrapped up his sermon with a prayer. I thanked God for the wisdom and hoped my high-mileage Hyundai would start again.

The engine sputtered and started humming. I smiled and turned the radio to some jazz. I eased back on the interstate, feeling more tolerant of how my journey through life was unfolding.

Chapter 6
EMERGENCY ROOM CLAMOR

THE EMERGENCY ROOM HAD NOT BEEN A CORDIAL OR friendly place—a bottomless pit in the night. There had been no coffee. The vending machines blinked empty. Horrible victims streamed in nonstop from the darkness outside.

A refined young doctor dressed in a white lab coat, jeans, and cowboy boots, emerged from the white curtain. On his heels trailed a nurse with youthful enthusiasm, her blond ponytail bouncing. She headed for Cal.

"Oh, honey, your brother looks like Peter O'Toole. He is so cute," the nurse said.

I was surprised she knew about Peter O'Toole.

The doctor frowned at her. "We are not sure what's

wrong. He needs exploratory surgery. He may live through surgery, or he may not," he said.

He was close to a coma. The nurse patted Cal on the arm. No movement.

I looked at my sister.

"We don't have another choice," my sister said. "He may die either way, so the best hope is surgery."

A tumor was removed, along with his appendix. He was sent to ICU. He lay motionless. I felt nervous and helpless. His life was hovering in the shadows. His skin was cold to the touch. I froze with fear every time I heard him cough. The nurse showed me how to use a suction tube that unblocked mucus from his throat. I kept tabs on the monitors and checked his pulse as if I knew what I was doing. No reaction from him. I felt as though I was in a cold, weightless fishbowl, not knowing what could be outside. I was weary. The long-drawn-out days melted my existence into mush. Immobilized.

Out of my gloom, I saw a sophisticated young gentleman dressed in jeans, leather cowboy boots, and a denim shirt. No white lab coat. He introduced himself as the attending doctor. I was so surprised by his attire I could hardly focus on what he was saying. Was he really the doctor? Was I dreaming? I was weary. Had I ended up in a Stephen King movie? I only longed for chocolate and a cup of coffee. He had neither.

He stood quiet and self-composed, which finally got my attention.

"Your brother needs to have a feeding tube," he said.

Was he serious? What was a feeding tube? Hadn't he already had enough tubes?

"I have to call my sister," I said. "Will it keep him alive?"

He explained that Cal couldn't eat enough food to keep him alive, so he would have liquid food going directly to his stomach.

My head swirled. I called my sister.

We gave him the authority to proceed.

The doctor nodded to the attendants. They lifted him on the gurney. His eyes fluttered. My stomach churned with every squeak of the gurney wheels when they took him away.

The doctor inserted one more tube, this time in his stomach. With all his tubes, he looked like an octopus. A regular room meant one step up in his recovery—back to the nursing home.

I drove home that night; glad Cal had gotten out of the prison of ICU. The full moon beamed down on the road. I tried to dismiss the chilling thought of the challenging future of aging Americans. There will be all this concern about recycling, global warming, and solar power but none about an aging population. The world will be unprepared and greedy. A nursing home will not be a haven. What will be happening to me? My children? My grandchildren?

Now I only hoped that the bad tire on my Hyundai would get me home.

Chapter 7

RUNAWAY FEEDING TUBE

I STOOD BY MY CAR THE NEXT MORNING. I STRETCHED AS IF the world had been taken off my shoulders. I looked toward the new nursing home. It was elaborate on the outside. Inside the doors, it felt like a scary dungeon. I gathered my courage and headed for the carved wooden doors. The smell of antiseptic hovered as I entered. The large silver coffee machine on the counter produced a smell of sweet coffee. Doughnuts were tucked beside it. I had a sudden need for a fresh cup of coffee. I wished Cal could have a cup. I kept moving, anxious to see how he was doing with the new feeding tube.

I entered Cal's room. The "liquid" from his feeding tube was running all over him, the bed, and dripping on the floor. Forget the red call light. I headed straight to the nurses' station. The overworked nurse looked up with a pleasant smile and listened intently. She rubbed her forehead. A phone rang in the distance. I wondered how many hours she had been there without a break.

"Cal needs help. His feeding tube is not functioning properly," I said. I hoped to be pleasant enough so she would help me.

She looked down at the stack of files as she spoke.

"No one will have time for him right now," she said. "Why don't you turn on the call light?"

A red call light didn't mean much. It only winked at people passing by. I told her I would fix the tube myself. She looked back to her stack of files and continued working.

I secretly had no idea what to do. Back at the room I started looking for something, anything that would give me a clue as to what to do. The liquid kept oozing. Cal seemed semi-aware of the mess. I took the tube that had been loose and held it up and decided to wrap it around the stand close to the liquid-filled bag. The oozing liquid stopped. I sighed, feeling a small sense of accomplishment.

Cal slept.

I heaved the 150-pound lifeless body over on his side. I tugged at the soaked sheets.

The nurse's aide sauntered in with the roommate's breakfast tray. She stopped and stared at Cal. Then me.

"What are you doing?" she asked.

I explained my dilemma.

"The nurse is going to be furious that you took charge of a feeding tube," she said.

"No one can help me. He's soaked. The liquid breakfast is everywhere. Can you get a person who can help me?" I asked.

She dropped the tray on the nightstand, spilling the orange juice, and rushed out. When the overworked nurse appeared, I didn't give her a chance to talk. I hoped I wasn't in trouble again.

"Get him an ambulance to take him back to the hospital. He needs a new tube," I said.

"We don't have an order for that," she said.

"Then I will call them myself," I said.

She backed away. "Don't do that. I'll see what I can do," she said.

I washed his face with a warm washcloth and pulled the covers over him. I allowed ten minutes for an answer.

I seethed.

Cal slept.

Bursting through the door came the angels of hope, those handsome paramedics with their strong muscles and compassion. I jumped in surprise.

They went straight to Cal's bed.

"What's up, guy?" they asked.

Cal blinked his eyes and waved at them.

They scooped him up, using the bedspread like a hammock, and put him on the gurney. They started toward the door.

"What about the bedspread?" I asked.

The passionate paramedics stopped and smiled at me.

"Don't worry. It's OK," a paramedic said.

My anger subsided. I grabbed my purse and followed them.

Back to the bottomless pit. Emergency room blues. I should have had a seat reserved for me. He was taken inside another black hole and emerged with a new tube. I wanted to stay with him at the hospital. The next day was Christmas. Any other year, we would have gathered, open gifts and ate a delicious meal. Tonight, I only sat and watched a semiconscious body and a small Christmas tree blink its tiny lights. I didn't know what his future would be or even mine.

"Cal, you have to get better," I said to him.

He didn't move. The room was cold. I wrapped my shawl tighter around my shoulders.

I laid my head on the foot of his bed and went to sleep.

Chapter 8
INDEPENDENCE DAY

THE SUN'S LUSTER SHIMMERED ACROSS THE ROOM. I struggled out of bed, dropped my feet to the floor. I wanted to help Cal get settled in the new nursing home. The feeding tube, like an umbilical cord, had been rolled on the transport with him to the facility. I couldn't take care of him at home. I hoped our money would last long enough to pay for his recovery. I had to trust God for help.

I stopped at Cal's door. I decided this would be a great day for him. He needed to be up in the wheelchair. I asked Joseph, his new aide, to get him up and prop him up with pillows. I entered the room with high hopes of a great recovery. We tried to wake him as we dressed him for a ride in his wheelchair. Cal's head hung, eyes closed, but he rode. *He will wake up soon,* I thought. I wished that with all my heart.

The administrator spotted us and rushed down the hall.

"Are you trying to kill him?" the administrator said. "Get him out of that wheelchair and back in bed."

"Leave him alone," I said.

I pushed the wheelchair past her as though she were invisible. That was bold of me. I always followed the rules. She frowned and left.

Now I was in trouble again.

"We can do this, Cal," I said. I hoped he could hear me.

Each time I came to the nursing home, I climbed over the feet of all the wheelchairs in the dayroom to get to Cal's wheelchair. The big-screen TV was always blaring. He had been sleeping in the chair. I detangled his chair from the others, pushing him to a separate room—the feeding room. He had to be spoon-fed. He didn't talk. He eyes only inched open and then closed. I spoon-fed him in tiny bites. He would hold the bites in his mouth and finally swallow. Some of it dribbled down his chin. His dining friend tried to give him some of her food. He swallowed a little of hers too.

On Saturday, a miracle happened.

"Give me that spoon," he said.

Startled, I dropped the spoon on the table. He reached for the spoon. His grasp was shaky and frail as he picked it up.

I clapped.

"You did it. I knew you could," I said.

Cal looked up with a twinkle in his eye. He slowly dipped his spoon into the mashed potatoes.

Chapter 9
ESCAPE

I WHEELED CAL OUTSIDE INTO THE UNPREDICTABLE TEXAS winter weather. I had wrapped blankets around him and taken him behind the nursing home by the large dryer vent. The warm air spewed out on us. We visited with the nurse's aides, who were taking a break and smoking. Cal drank his coffee—a highlight of his day.

Cal had begun making friends. Three lady friends, who could walk, were trying to find their rooms. They had gone to several rooms asking if they lived there. Cal wanted to go with them.

They stopped in in the doorway of Room 12.

"Do we live here?" one asked.

A screechy voice came from the dark room. "This one is full."

They frowned and pointed to Room 13. We followed.

"Does Amy live here?" another asked.

The voice from this room sounded like a rusty hinge. "No, she does not live here."

The friends seemed stunned and confused. They sat down on the hall bench and looked around. Cal wanted to sit next to them. No one spoke. It was winding down time, as the darkness hovered outside. The aide finally noticed them and put them all to bed. I left with a heavy heart.

The next morning, I arrived after their breakfast. I was rested and anticipated a wonderful day. I started down the hall to Cal's room.

His aide followed me with a walkie-talkie. "We can't find your brother," he said.

I swallowed a big lump in my throat. "Can't find my brother? What do you mean?" I asked. "Why didn't you call me?"

I dashed to his room. The aide followed. Cal's clothes were still in the closet. We whirled through each hall, the TV room, the physical therapy room, and the cafeteria. We combed through each bush outside, the parking lot, and even looked down the road. Cal was nowhere to be seen. *He couldn't have gone far in a wheelchair,* I thought. My fear and anxiety were now gripping my stomach. I had to sit down on the wooden bench out back in the shade. I put my head in my hands and bent over. He was doing so well; had he planned an escape?

"Cal, Cal, I need you. Come back," I said.

The aide stood motionless, staring at me. Minutes seemed like hours.

The truck driver had propped the door open to the cafeteria to take boxes of vegetables inside from his truck. I heard a voice come from the other side of the truck.

My heart skipped a beat. Cal? I headed for the sound of the voice. Cal? He was waiting for someone, but not me. I checked the brake on his chair and looked for scratches and cuts. He was secure. Who should I have been angry with—the caretakers, Cal, or the truck driver? I blocked my anger and hugged him. Thank God for small miracles.

"What are you doing out here by yourself?" I asked.

"I want to go home. The driver is taking me home," Cal said.

"Calm down. He doesn't know the way to your house," I said.

He looked up meekly from under his baseball cap. "Then I want to go home with you," he said.

Stunned and speechless, I caught my breath searching for the right answer. "OK, let's let Joseph put you in my car, and we'll ride around," I said.

He looked at me with sadness in his eyes.

I longed to take him home, but I couldn't lift him. He needed twenty-four-hour care.

The ride might ease his heartache and mine too, I thought. I hoped he would forget the idea.

"Let's go get coffee," I said.

He perked up, lifting his head, at the sound of coffee.

We returned to Sonic and got our coffees. He

focused on the warm sunshine coming into the car window. The fresh spring air floated around us, and we rode back. He beamed.

I wondered if he had been planning his next escape.

Chapter 10
RED CALL LIGHTS

IT WAS 6:45 P.M.

I flipped the red call light switch for help.

By 7:45 p.m., no one. Not enough staff.

Red call lights lit the hall. Nurses' aides had been running in and out of rooms.

Cal was waiting patiently in his wheelchair. "Why are they taking so long?" he asked.

I checked the deserted hall again. No one.

He wore a wet adult diaper. His clothes were soiled from dinner. I heard him wheezing.

"Can't breathe," Cal said.

He struggled for another breath.

Frantic, I jumped from my chair, almost turned over

the bed tray, and stubbed my toe on the bed frame. I hobbled to the door and looked down the deserted hall. Had the call light shorted out? I raced back to the nightstand. I dumped the contents of the drawer on the bed and frantically dug through the assortment of junk.

"Where is your inhaler?" I asked.

Cal looked up, frowning.

"The lady," Cal said. He pointed to the door.

"Oh no. The medication nurse has it locked in her cart," I said.

Grabbing the handles of the wheelchair, I hurried out the door. Cal's roommate called out to us.

Cal tried to answer but produced only a whisper.

I ignored the exchange and kept him moving. I wished I had worn my tennis shoes.

The empty hall displayed red call lights blinking at almost every door. I knew that a medication nurse had been working in another hall. We headed in that direction.

Cal gasped for another breath. He pointed to a cart. I saw an athletic, well-groomed silhouette putting medicine in tiny cups.

"Look," Cal said.

I pressed harder against the wheelchair handles, forcing it to move faster.

"Help us. Cal can't breathe, and no one is in our hall to help," I said.

Her eyes exhibited panic. She locked up the cart. "Let's go," she said.

Her strong hands grabbed the wheelchair. She

spun him around like he was on a carnival ride. We scrambled back to our hall. It was deserted. Call lights blinked like Christmas tree decorations.

She paused, observed the blinking lights, and frowned.

"I wonder what all these patients need?" she asked.

What an unanswerable question, I thought.

"I have no idea," I said. "Can you please give him a breathing treatment?"

She ignored me. Her strong voice boomed. "Where is everyone?"

The exasperated aide, his eyes wide, looked startled as he ran down the hall, napkin in his hand, wiping his face.

Cal huffed with all the strength he could muster to talk to them. "Can't breathe," he said.

The aide froze at the sight of Cal and hurried away. The medication nurse was nipping at his heels.

"Wait. Bring his breathing machine," I called out.

Two minutes seemed like two hours before a nurse appeared. "We are on break," she said. "What's going on here?"

"Everyone is on break?" I asked. "I think we have a serious problem."

I shouldn't have said that.

She frowned and ignored my comment. I was in trouble again.

Cal was wheezing.

She grabbed the wheelchair and rushed Cal into his room.

She started toward the door.

I felt that everyone had been abandoning us.

"What about Cal?" I asked.

She kept walking.

"Please bring his breathing machine, and I will give him the treatment myself," I said.

Cal struggled for more breath. He looked more distressed with every passing minute.

I tried to get my panic and anger under control. I wasn't sure what I would have said to anyone who returned. I tried to keep calm. Had I been asking too much or just asking the wrong person?

"They will be back in a matter of seconds," I said.

Cal kept wheezing. Breathless.

I trembled.

Without a word, a lanky girl wearing a butterfly print scrub top rushed in and almost dropped the breathing machine on the nightstand. She filled it with medication and plugged it in. The old machine grumbled and finally started. She smiled at me and pushed back her long silky black hair from her forehead.

She left as quickly as she had come.

I grabbed the attached mask and secured it on Cal's face. He gasped for the lifesaving mist. Safe now.

The lumpy chair beside his bed caught me. I only wished I could have been a better caretaker.

Had I been doing the right thing?

Chapter 11

CAR RIDE

CAL'S SHINY, BLACK 1924 MODEL T FORD WAS SITTING in the driveway. Cal hurried out. He was seventeen and had worked at the feed store to buy his vintage dream car. The screen backdoor slammed shut behind him. I ran after him.

"I want to go with you," I said.

He turned around, looked at me, and mumbled. "Oh no, not again. Do I have to take my little sister everywhere?"

I ran ahead of him and jumped on the running board of the car, waiting for an answer.

Cal put his hands on his hips. "Get in, but you have to sit down and leave the door handles alone," he said.

I smiled, hoping he wouldn't change his mind. I climbed in and smoothed out my dress. I wondered if

I was dressed nicely enough. Cal wore his favorite blue shirt and best jeans, which I'd seen him ironing earlier. He closed my door and smiled.

He lifted one side of the hood and checked the four spotless spark plugs he'd cleaned earlier. Looking over the engine, he closed the hood, grabbed the crank from the floorboard, and walked to the front of the car. He put the crank in the front grill to start the engine. Restless, I waited, peering through the large, flat windshield he'd just cleaned. I felt so grown up.

"Is it going to start this time?" I asked.

He looked up, annoyed. He turned the crank again. A growl emerged from the under hood. Then silence.

I gave a sigh.

He glared at me and turned the crank more vigorously.

A loud, peaceful hum came from underneath the hood. He smiled, ran to the driver's side door, and tossed the crank back inside. He jumped in and put his feet on the pedals. He released one pedal, and we started rolling backward out of the driveway. *How did he do that?* I wondered?

"I think it's going to stop running now," I said.

He gripped the steering wheel harder and edged the car forward.

"This is a fine old car. It will go forty-five miles an hour. I wish I could go faster though," he said.

What a smooth ride.

I heard barking behind us.

"Stop, stop. Dotty is following us," I said.

Cal looked at me and frowned. "I don't have time for this. Maybe she'll give up," he said.

Dotty kept coming after us. Cal pulled a lever and stopped the car, leaning us forward. He sat motionless, gritting his teeth.

I jumped out, wrapped my arms around Dotty, and stood outside the car door.

I wouldn't dare get in. I thought I might have to walk back home. I crossed my fingers and waited for him to say get in.

It felt like a lifetime had passed before he spoke.

"OK. She can go this time, but you have to hold her tight because she might jump out," he said.

I put Dotty in the seat, jumped in, and held her tight.

Cal eased the pedals again, and the tapping engine move us faster.

The skinny black spoke wheels of the black Ford rolled us into the small hometown. He drove on the red brick street looking for the turn to the post office and grocery store. Cal's friend waved at us from the front door of the hardware store. Cal waved back and honked the horn, which sounded like a duck squawking. Cal's flaming red hair danced in the breeze, and his blue eyes sparkled. Dotty rode. The sun streamed in the open window and warmed my face. *Can there be anything better?* I thought. What a great car. We came to a stop in front of the old, red brick post office.

"Wait here. I must get stamps for Mama. Don't touch anything," he said.

"I promise," I said.

Cal eased out of the car. The car idled as I held Dotty

tighter. I gazed off into the baby blue sky. The clouds floated like giant marshmallows. I jumped when Cal spoke.

"Now let's stop by the grocery store to get my chewing tobacco," he said.

He pulled levers and pushed foot pedals. How did he do that? We nestled up to the curb in front of the store where our aunt worked. She waved from inside the large plate-glass window. Cal turned off the engine.

"Wait here. And as I said, don't go anywhere," he said.

I pushed Dotty closer. I was tired of sitting but had to stay put if I ever wanted to go again. He returned quickly with his tobacco. My aunt followed him. Her white apron was starched and spotless. She gave me a chocolate and petted Dotty. Cal grabbed the crank again. The engine started effortlessly. Cal honked. I waved at my aunt. Dotty barked.

"Can you teach me how to drive?" I asked.

Cal continued to drive, looking straight ahead.

"I sure can, and someday you can take me for a ride."

Chapter 12
CARE PLAN DISASTER

I FELT DANGER ALL AROUND ME. AS I ENTERED THE LOBBY, the supervisor approached me.

"There is a care plan meeting today at 2:00. You be there," she said.

She walked away.

I was sure the meeting was about Cal's bruises. Maybe I was in trouble. I was always saying something I shouldn't.

Nurses' aides didn't speak to me when I pushed Cal into the cafeteria for lunch. They skirted around us doling out the unappetizing food. I dug to the bottom of my tote for snacks I brought him from home. I found the avocado and special cheese sticks he liked. The aides moved on when I asked for a coffee refill for

Cal. Their demeanor gave me a clue of what might be coming in the meeting.

I felt protection having Cal with me as I went into the meeting to face the administrator and her crew. My stomach churned.

We sat.

"Do you have anything to say before we begin?" she asked.

The two aides looked daggers my way. I knew then that the meeting was, perhaps, not entirely about Cal's health.

"Yes, I do. What did I do that makes you all so angry with me?" I asked.

No one answered.

Shattering the silence, the administrator blurted out. "You made the statement that your brother is being hit by the employees," she said.

I stared back at them, trying to process the statement. Our eyes locked. I gathered my thoughts.

"I didn't blame anyone. I voiced my concerns here on Friday about his bruises. No one seemed to know anything about it, and the stories keep changing," I said.

"Someone called me at my house complaining about the bruises. They also said that you refused a breathing treatment for him," she said.

What irrational statements, I thought. My hands grasped the chair arms.

"I would never refuse a breathing treatment for him; besides, he is the only one who can refuse one," I said.

She nervously shuffled the papers in front of her.

"Someone called the state about your brother," she said.

The tension simmered. The aides sat quietly. The small, windowless room seemed to be suffocating me. The wooden clock ticking on the wall sounded like a tower clock clanging out to the city. I imagined the clock to be ticking out the time for my execution. A blanket of silence hovered, smothering the room.

Cal broke the silence. "Let's go," he said.

I had heartfelt gratitude for his rescue. Cal was usually not very responsive to anything.

I maneuvered the wheelchair out from the table, not giving them a second look. The heavy door slammed shut behind us.

"We're safe," I said.

Cal waved his hands as if to say keep moving.

Carol, the head nurse, ran after us down the hall. I told her everything.

"Well, I'm not making excuses for us, but that was gossip that escalated. You should still voice your concerns because you are here to watch out after your brother. I'll be watching too," she said.

Cal gave a frustrated sigh and got involved, leaning forward in his wheelchair. "Izzie, you should just leave this alone," he said.

Surprised at his alertness, I paid attention. "Cal, we have just begun."

Cal waved his hand. We moved on outside for fresh air.

Chapter 13
MISSING TEETH

I LOOKED OUT THE WINDOW, TRYING TO BE POSITIVE. THE view was a harsh red brick wall, skinny mesquite trees, abundant cactus, and a dried-up watering tank not far away.

"I know a fantastic place outside," I said.

Cal looked at me, trying to wake up.

I pushed his wheelchair to the only spot of beauty, the towering trees on the other side of the building. I locked the wheels. We rested in the shade, enjoying the warm breeze and watching birds swirl close by. I counted my blessings. *What a good day this is.*

I interrupted the peaceful moment. "I brought you a snack," I said.

Cal looked inquisitive when I rummaged in my

tote for his favorite cheddar cheese and crackers. He reached for the white paper bag I handed him.

"Don't have my false teeth," he said.

I grasped the bag back, trying to curb my horror.

"Who has your teeth?" I asked. "We just got you new ones."

He looked up into the blue sky. "Don't know," he said.

"How did you eat your breakfast?" I asked.

"Don't know."

"Let's go inside right now," I said.

I pushed the wheelchair through the sculptured lawn into the carved wood front door. The supervisor's office was the first door. She'd tagged me as a troublemaker, so I was sure I'd cause more trouble. I wheeled Cal into the office. I knew I had to be calm.

"Someone has his new false teeth," I said. "I'm sure he couldn't eat breakfast this morning. You need to help me find them or get him some new ones."

She was startled.

"Let's go look," she said. "He probably just took them out and left them somewhere."

She rolled her chair back and frowned.

I followed her, trying to camouflage my unfriendly thoughts.

"He would never leave his teeth anywhere. He was proud of his new teeth," I said.

She ignored me.

We looked under the bed, shook the bed covers, and checked the drawers. I pulled open the top drawer. His new watch was missing from the back of the drawer.

My anger smoldered inside me like a volcano ready to erupt. I curbed the anger.

"His watch is gone too," I said.

She scowled at my news.

"Are you sure?" she asked.

I continued to pull out his belongings.

"Yes, you have to file a report," I said.

She shrugged and headed for the door.

"I'll see if any aides or residents have them," she said.

I was thinking that none of the residents have the items, as they seemed to be always sleeping.

Cal watched her leave.

"I'll find your teeth. You watch is probably gone forever. I'm sorry," I said.

Cal shook his head in dismay.

Our next stop was the cafeteria manager asking to have his food pureed. I told all the residents' families I met, hoping they might have discovered the teeth somewhere.

"We can get some soft food you don't have to chew, and we'll wait," I said.

We waited.

The next day at 5:00 p.m., there was a soft knock at the door. The fashionable front desk receptionist appeared with something wrapped in a paper towel. She held the paper towel in a stylish manner like an elegant gift. Her red high heels clicked on the tile floor as she came over to give me the paper towel.

"I just found these teeth in my desk drawer," she

said. "I heard about Cal. These may be his. I have no idea how they got there."

She carefully handed me the teeth and waited. I thought that must have taken a lot of courage for her to come carrying teeth from her desk drawer.

"Thank you. It's worth a try to see if they fit," I said.

Cal perked up.

I cleaned and sanitized them for an exceptionally long time. Should I have let him try these on? They looked like his new ones. I took a chance. I handed them to Cal. He put them in his mouth.

He smiled.

They fit.

Chapter 14
PEP TALK

TODAY I WAS APPREHENSIVE ABOUT GOING TO THE nursing home. *Why am I giving up everything to take care of someone?* My mind floated. How foolish of me to think that. I needed a self-pep talk.

I hadn't given up walks in the park. Stars, moon, sun, clouds, and flowers would always be available. I still had my books, pen and paper, my cat, kids, grandkids, great-grandkids, and my genuine friend. I had gas money. Best of all, I hadn't had to give up my brother. I was sure I could think of other things as I drove.

I headed out the door with a spark in my heart.

Chapter 15
THE SHOWER

THE ROADSIDE MESQUITE TREES SHOWED OFF THEIR GREEN leaves in the middle of the brown, deserted plains. I listened to the radio and finished my coffee. I pushed the car to eighty. I couldn't afford new tires or a ticket. Besides that, I was tired. I eased the car to sixty and took my time. My anxiety was building.

I pulled into the well-manicured grounds of the one-story, newly built nursing home. If people only knew what went on inside, compared to the stunning brick outside. I wondered what I would find this Sunday.

Inside the main lobby, I discovered an empty receptionist desk. The nurses' station was stacked with charts. I was sure the nurse was away, trying to take care of her seventy-five patients. The aides were lounging around the counter. I said good morning.

No one answered. Not a good sign. The deserted halls could have been used as a bowling alley.

Cal was sleeping when I entered the room. The smell of urine took my breath away. Stepping closer, I saw he had on wet pajamas. His sheets looked like an ocean wave had washed over them. It was 10:00 a.m., and obviously no one had been in to check on him.

How could this happen?

Had he had breakfast?

I turned on the "never beckoning" call light, checked to be sure it worked, and turned back inside to the smell in the room.

"Wake up, Cal." I shook his shoulder.

No response.

Was he drugged?

"Cal?"

I had to do something.

Help had to come soon.

I searched the room for gloves. Nothing there.

I resembled an ant trying to move a big rock. I heaved him over trying to take the wet clothes off my sleeping brother.

The roommate's daughter entered the room and saw that her dad was also soaked and sleeping. She dropped her purse on the floor and started pacing.

"I'm going to report this neglect to the supervisor," she said.

I frowned.

"Be careful what you say. Your dad might get mistreated when you are not here," I said.

She pushed her glasses down and looked over the

rims. "No, he won't," she said. She moved back slightly rising an eyebrow.

"I just wanted to help you," I said.

I dropped Cal's urine-soaked blanket in a plastic bag.

An aide strolled in talking on his cell phone. He looked at both of us, put his cell phone in his pocket, and started helping us. We all three struggled together to remove the wet pajamas, sheets, and pillowcases. The aide put the soiled pajamas and linens in a laundry bag. We handed him clean clothes from the drawers. The men slept, making the process even more exhausting.

The aide struggled to get Cal lifted into the wheelchair. He propped his head up.

"Cal needs a bath," I said.

"He doesn't get a bath on Sunday," he said. "It's not in his schedule."

I gripped the wheelchair handles tighter.

"OK, then I will put him, wheelchair and all, in the shower. I know you have a shower chair, but I can't lift him in. I need to get all this smell off him," I said.

He left. The roommate's daughter followed him out.

"Come on, Cal. Let's get you a shower," I said.

He was drowsy. His head drooped. *That's not like him,* I thought. I pushed the wheelchair out the door to find the shower. Passing by each door, I found a door marked "Shower." I knocked.

No one there.

I backed him in while trying to hold the door open with my foot.

Finally, in.

I turned him around and discovered, to my surprise, the shower was as big as the room.

I parked the wheelchair under the showerhead, locked the wheels, and took off my shoes.

Clean fluffy towels and washcloths were waiting behind the large cabinet doors. I tugged his shirt over his head. Grabbing the pajama pants at the hem, I pulled and tugged. Sweat poured down my face. That will have to do I thought. I started toward the shower knobs. I didn't care if we both got soaked. At least, he would be clean.

"Here comes the water," I said. "Hold your soap and washcloth tight."

Feeling the warm water on him, he slowly rubbed his chest with the soap.

He spoke in a whisper. "Feels good," he said

"You are going to be clean in here, if nothing else," I said.

Just as I finished soaping his feet, three people dressed in uniforms appeared in the door. One was the supervisor.

"Oh, great, Cal. Now we have stirred up trouble again," I said.

He ignored me and continued to enjoy the luxury of the shower.

The supervisor folded her arms and tapped her foot on the wet tiles.

She pointed to me. "Look at her," she said. "She's not allowed here."

I looked up at her. A rockslide of anger tumbled

inside of me. The aides stared at us, trying to avoid the spray of the shower.

I harnessed my feelings. *Keep calm,* I told myself.

"He has not had a bath in three days. I know because I have been here. He was soaked in urine this morning, and the aide couldn't bathe him," I said.

She unfolded her arms and looked at Cal, who was soaked and smiling.

"Oh then, get out of here. I will see that the aides finish," she said. She sent a warning with her eyes.

"I still think you are the one who called the state," she said.

Standing by Cal's chair, I looked straight at her. "I didn't, but give me the number," I said.

No one moved.

Cal smiled as I waved to him and left the shower.

Chapter 16
BASEBALL

A FEELING OF HOPELESSNESS LINGERED. I FELT CLOSE TO checking into the nursing facility myself. I had an idea that might take Cal and I away from the monotony, stress, and grief of the nursing home. A Texas Ranger Baseball Stadium tour seemed exciting enough.

John, the aide, knew we were going. He put on Cal's favorite shirt—a denim shirt that matched his deep blue eyes. His stomach had swollen so large that he could only tug on sweats two sizes too big. Cal frowned as John put the brown house shoes on his swollen feet.

"I know you want your boots, but they don't fit right now," I said.

Cal smiled when I rolled him to the lobby in his

wheelchair headed toward the door. He was getting to go somewhere.

"Wait! Wait!" said the nurse running after us. "Here is his inhaler and medicine."

I swallowed, took a deep breath, and stopped. What if she hadn't caught us? She was overworked again today. She gave him his medicine and handed me the inhaler.

The city shuttle I scheduled was pulling into the drive. The driver ignored distractions. He stepped out and opened the wheelchair ramp. He nodded and smiled as he buckled Cal in his wheelchair on the ramp. The warm breeze circled us. What a beautiful spring day. As the shuttle ramp lifted Cal up, I wished both of us would be immersed in a bucket of happiness. The driver, paying attention to every detail, rolled Cal and his chair into the shuttle with amazing efficiency.

I stared out the large shuttle window, mesmerized by the stately red brick structure of Texas Stadium up ahead. It contained black steel and wraparound granite. I marveled at the carvings in the granite that depicted scenes from Texas history. Our driver meticulously unloaded Cal from the shuttle ramp and rolled him onto the sidewalk of the lush, green landscape. Cal leaned forward in his chair and seemed to take in all the splendor.

"Look, there's the Alamo carved in the granite over there," I said.

I pointed. He looked up. I wasn't sure he could focus on it. He sat, without a word, trying to savor the experience.

I bought our tickets. We entered the enormously empty stadium overlooking the baseball field. I felt swallowed up by its size. An eerie quietness surrounded us.

Our tour began with an enthusiastic guide.

"The field grass is real. There is Bermuda grass in the summer and ryegrass in the winter. It has to be mowed every day," he said.

"Cal, would you like to mow that?" I asked. "We would have to get you a bigger mower."

He smiled.

"The upper-level tickets are forty-nine dollars and included in the price is all you can eat," the tour guide said.

I knew Cal enjoyed eating. He leaned forward, displaying a wide grin.

"Maybe we can go see a game," I said.

He nodded.

Our next stop was the press box. I struggled to get the wheelchair from the elevator. My heart was pounding. My face was red. I examined the heavy press box door. The tour guide opened it, and we all peered inside. It would be a struggle for me to get Cal inside. But thank goodness there was a guardian angel. A young tourist, with muscles, was part of our tour group. He courteously stepped forward.

"May I?" he asked.

He skillfully wheeled Cal inside. Cal gazed out the enormous windows of the press box. The field resembled a glistening green diamond. Cal tilted forward with a smile on his face when he heard the story about the lady who had once played the organ in the press box. The organ music was now only a recording.

Observing the suites will be smooth, I thought. We packed in the elevator with our group and emerged out into a beautifully decorated hall displaying elaborate doors. Cal gasped with surprise. We passed the President George W. Bush Suite.

"Don't think we'll be visiting this one," I said.

He smiled. We didn't get to go in.

Next, the Sample Suite. There was room for ten people. We squeezed in and immersed ourselves in another amazing view of the field. I didn't know how much Cal was absorbing, but it had to be more cheerful than the nursing home. I certainly had a new sense of being somewhat normal.

"Wow, Cal. Do you think they'll let us move in here?" I asked.

He shook his head no. At least, I thought, he was aware and perhaps forgetting about his illness for a while, but he was saying little.

Down the elevator again to the weight room and batting cages. I was getting better at wrestling with the elevator. The cages were built large enough for a small dinosaur. They were indestructible and reminded me of how fast a ball can be thrown and hit.

We moved on to the dugouts. I stood at the top of the steep steps, staring down uneasily below. I felt helpless.

"We'll wait up here," I said. "I can't get you down to the dugouts."

Cal waved his hand.

Our guardian angel appeared again. "You go down to the dugouts. I'll stay here for you," he said.

"Oh no, I can't do that," I said. "You won't get to see the dugouts, and Cal sure can't."

He laughed. "You go and then tell him about it. I will go when you get back," he said.

He motioned for me to go down into the dugout. Cal nodded knowingly.

I hurriedly exited down the steep stairs. I sat down and caught my breath. What an honor to have sat where a Texas Ranger had just sat the night before. I felt as though I had been part of the game. I only wished Cal could have sat with me.

I emerged energized and thanked our angel profusely.

"Now, Cal, I will get you a Ranger baseball cap and jersey," I said.

"Naaw," he said.

That meant no.

I continued to roll him toward the gift shop.

"It's a must have," I said.

He seemed overwhelmed viewing the rows of red, white, and blue shirts in the shop. He didn't comment, so I picked a red hat and matching jersey. I put the hat on his head. Still no comment from him. That meant he liked it. I paid for them before he had a chance to say no. I handed him the bag with the shirt. He neatly folded it and put it in his lap.

I called our shuttle to let them know we were finished. We waited out front, looking back at the miraculous place we had been. A yellow cab, labeled handicap, stopped near us. The driver called out Cal's name from his window.

"That's us. Where's the shuttle?" I asked.

"This is all the space we have right now. I'll put him in," he said.

"But he requires a caretaker to go with him. I need to go," I said.

The driver looked puzzled. "I'll take care of him. I do this all the time. We don't have any more room in this cab. We're busy. You can take the next cab that's coming right behind us," he said.

I had a little trust for the driver but felt uneasy letting Cal go with complete strangers.

"You will have to take responsibility for him if you take him in your cab," I said.

Cal's eyes sparkled as he saw the other two passengers. They were in wheelchairs too.

"I take handicapped patients all the time. I have it under control," the driver said.

I knew the drivers were careful, so I motioned for him to go even though I had mixed feelings. After all, it was only a fifteen-minute trip. I waved at Cal as they pulled away, and I waited for the other cab. I stopped worrying because I thought I would be right behind him.

Wrong.

I arrived at the nursing home first. I waited outside for Cal's cab. I paced up and down the front sidewalk. After fifteen minutes, I started to think they must have had a wreck, someone got sick and they went to the ER, or they let him off at the wrong place. I called the shuttle service. They couldn't reach the driver. I was petrified. I regretted my decision. I felt an onset of nausea and sat down exhausted on the front bench. I couldn't believe what I had done. I pressed my hands to my temples and considered calling 9-1-1. After another fifteen minutes of torturous waiting, my heart leaped as I saw a cab pull up. Someone in the cab had on a red baseball cap.

That's Cal.

I ran with a sudden burst of energy to the cab door and hurled my disappointment at the driver. "Where have you been?" I asked.

The radio was blaring. The passengers were all talking and laughing.

The driver yelled over the sound of the radio. "Oh, I had a drop-off and pickup at the last minute. It took a little more time," he said.

He opened the handicap ramp as if nothing unusual had happened and rolled Cal out.

Cal was displaying a wide grin and waving goodbye to his buddies.

Maybe it was a successful trip after all.

Chapter 17
TORNADO

THE SKY LOOKED TURBULENT. HEAVY, DARK CLOUDS loomed. I got in my car. The skies seemed clear enough to go. It would only be an hour drive, I thought. I was aware of dangerous wall clouds that held tornadoes. If there was a tornado warning on the radio, I would turn around.

Satisfied as I drove, I drank my coffee from my favorite Yeti cup and listened to the radio. A cloud sent a downpour. I slowed down, not being able to see much of the road. *Just a much-needed rain,* I thought. I listened to the rhythm of the rain as I finished my drive.

Before getting out of the car, I gave myself another pep talk. My nursing home anxiety, as I called it, was building. Running with my tattered umbrella, I struggled to get in the heavy glass door. Nurse Carol hurried to open the door for me. She was tall, refined, and spoke with a gentleness.

"There's a tornado warning. What in the world are you doing out?" she asked.

I panicked. How did I miss that news?

"What are you going to do about the residents? How's Cal?" I asked. "We grew up going to a storm shelter below ground when this happens. Did you tell him? Was he afraid?"

"He's fine," Nurse Carol said. Her smile was filled with warmth.

I anxiously scanned the deserted hall to Cal's room. I noticed that everyone was in their usual routine as if nothing were wrong. I calmed myself so not to upset Cal. I entered his room trying to smile. I sat down and quietly got his snack out of my tote. I had brought watermelon and waffle potato chips.

Cal took the chips and smiled. One of his favorites. He had on a clean blue shirt, oversize sweatpants, and warm red socks. He seemed not to be aware of the weather.

"I'll get you some coffee," I said.

I hoped when I left the room, I could get another weather report from someone. No one was in the hall. I didn't linger. The TV in the cafeteria blared. We were in a red zone. That meant a tornado had been sighted by radar near us. Not good. I was not prepared for this. Fear was tightening my throat.

I grabbed a cup of coffee and hurried away from the large glass windows in the abandoned cafeteria. The gruesome clouds were now boiling with lightning. The wind was getting stronger.

This didn't look good. The tornado was hovering close.

My heart pounded. I entered Cal's room.

Cal pointed to the window. "Storm," he said.

Now he knows. I must get him away from the windows.

Suddenly, the city weather siren screamed outside, letting us know a tornado was coming. The sunny day turned to dark gray. Trees were bending over as their leaves were being snatched away by the angry wind. I felt I might die from a heart attack even before the tornado got close. Cal looked at me. I realized I had to go into survival mode and react in a position of control.

An announcement boomed through the speakers. "Get out into the hall everyone. Stay there."

I sat the coffee down, splashing it on the tray table and the floor. I gripped the handles of Cal's wheelchair and pushed him out into the hall, leaving my purse, car keys, and cell phone. I wanted them. Who needed them now? I didn't go back. Cal held the chips tighter. I closed his door. I told him the hall was a safe place. I wished I believed that and there had been another choice.

Nurses and aides started maneuvering residents. Two aides pushed a bed with a patient in it out through the door. Wheelchairs merged like five o'clock traffic. Other residents walked slowly with their canes as if they were on an afternoon stroll. A hush came over the crowded hall. I wondered what the residents were thinking. How many storms had they been through? How many times in their life had they experienced this unfavorable dilemma? Did they wish they were home? They appeared dignified and calm in anticipation. Everyone exchanged looks.

I clung to Cal's wheelchair with every muscle. What kind of protection was this from a tornado? We were all helpless bystanders.

I placed my hands firmly on Cal's shoulders. Was this my only way to protect him? He tucked the chips into the side of the wheelchair and placed his hands as tightly as he could around the wheelchair arms. He looked down. I recalled shocking images I had seen on TV of stores and houses being snatched away by a tornado. I felt powerless. Trapped. I had to trust God now.

The hail cut through the air without warning and pounded on the roof as if wanting in. It cracked windows. The wind blew like a dragon's breath out of control. The building shook. I heard the shattering of glass. Moving through was a deafening sound like a freight train coming through the building. I froze. No one said a word. No one screamed. Sweeping in was an eerie hush outside. I felt petrified in a vacuum. Smells of garlic from dinner, rubbing alcohol, and perspiration circled around us. No one moved. Was there more to come? I was struggling to speak but couldn't. Cal didn't move.

The lights flickered.

Soon the sound of helicopter rotor blades swirled overhead. What a beautiful sound. *We're in the clear,* I told myself. The rain now fell softly, washing away the nightmare.

"We made it through," I said.

My heart stopped pounding.

I let go of Cal.

Cal looked up, relaxing his posture.

The residents began their usual chatter.

"Can I have my coffee now?" Cal asked.

"Of course," I said.

I started to move. I felt the heaviness lifted from my muscles.

Nurse Carol came wearily down the crowded hall weaving in and out of wheelchairs. She nervously shuffled the papers on her clipboard.

"We were on the edge of the tornado. It's gone. We're so lucky," she said.

She stared at me. "You can't go home now. A gas station has been demolished. A semitruck was lifted into the sky and dropped five miles away. Luckily, no one was inside the truck. There's debris everywhere. You can stay here. I'll get you a blanket," she said.

She walked away, heading for the linen closet.

I welcomed a warm blanket and a worn-out nursing home chair.

Chapter 18

COTTON FIELD FLASHBACK

A THIRTY-MINUTE DRIVE TO GRANDADDY'S FARM WOULD take us down the mountain. We would pass the green mesquite trees of late spring. I looked forward to the explosion of color made by the West Texas wildflowers in full bloom.

"Get in the car," Mama called to Cal. "We're going to your grandaddy's farm. We need some money. Now that you're fourteen you can pick lots of cotton in a day and make us some money."

"I won't have to do housework today," Cal said.

He rushed to the old Ford.

"Is Izzie going with us? She is kind of too young to pick," Cal said.

Mama pointed and Cal went to the flowerbed of hibiscus looking for me.

"Come on out before she changes her mind," he coaxed.

I crawled out of the yellow flowering bushes, anxious to see what was happening. I followed him to the car. Mama stood in the back door with her bottle of cough medicine and a spoon.

"Wait until I take my medicine. Then we'll go," she said.

The wooden screen door slammed behind her as she headed toward our old black Ford.

She wiped her forehead and mumbled. "Must be a hundred today. This old Ford better not heat up again," she said.

"Don't worry, Mama. I can try to fix it for you," Cal boasted.

The scorching wind soared through the car. We had rolled down the windows, giving us some relief from the heat. The hot puffs of wind pulled at my long hair and straightened the curls Mama had made. Cal sat peacefully in the front looking out at the countryside. The wind whisked through his red hair. His deep blue eyes glistened. He was wearing his well-worn shoes, sleeveless denim shirt, and faded jeans that were frayed at the bottom.

The scorching ride took us to the white frame country house. The sturdy wooden barn loft was filled with square bales of hay. Tall elm and bushy mesquite trees filled the smooth, rolling hills. My grandmother ran down the steps from the wraparound porch. Her exquisite black dress with a white crochet collar flowed in the wind. Her shiny, gray hair was expertly twisted into a bun.

She gracefully reached for the door handle and opened the car door for us. Her welcoming smile warmed me.

"Cal, your uncle is coming to get you to take you to the field," she said.

Mama gave that stern look.

"Oh, Izzie is going with him too," she said.

Grandmother looked puzzled. Her smile faded.

"She's too young. She doesn't know how to pick cotton. She—"

Mama interrupted her. "She can learn."

Grandmother gave a sigh of resignation, helped us out of the car, and took us to the kitchen. The aroma of fresh cooked sausage grabbed me. She wrapped the sausage and biscuits in a cloth for us to take to the cotton field. She filled a ceramic jug with water and handed it to Cal.

My uncle arrived outside driving a green tractor that transmitted a loud tapping noise. A large wooden wagon was attached. The wooden wheels on the wagon stirred up a whirlwind of dust. We swallowed the flakes of dust as we ran and jumped on the back of the wagon.

A captivating smile glowed from under my uncle's well-groomed black mustache. His straw hat, blue denim shirt, and khaki pants looked as if they had just come from a department store window.

He pointed to the front of the wagon.

"There's your bags for the cotton Cal. Take care of your little sis," he said.

Cal gathered the bags. We rode to the back of the cotton field. The wagon jerked to a halt. The jolt snapped me backward. I gripped the sides, fearing I would fall off. I reached for Cal.

He grabbed my arm as my uncle reached back, hoping to help rescue me.

"I have to go into town for more supplies, so I won't be able to come back for you," he said.

"That's OK. We'll walk back," Cal said.

I stood reluctantly and watched him disappear in a cloud of dust.

Cal motioned to me. "Let's go to work. I can teach you."

I followed.

He carried a large white bag for the cotton he would pick and handed me a small white bag. I held it in my arms. It itched.

Cal bent over to one of the four-foot bushy plants.

"See the fuzzy cotton in this brown crust. Pull the fuzz out and put it in the bag," he said.

The fuzz looked like white cotton candy. I pulled out the soft, fluffy fuzz and held it to my nose. There was no smell. I touched it to my tongue. No taste.

"Don't eat it," Cal snapped.

I frowned at him. I was disappointed that it wasn't something good to eat. I put the fuzz in my bag.

Cal's cotton bag stretched five feet behind him. He put the strap over his head and laid it across his chest. I glanced around to see a woman dressed in blue overalls and a plaid shirt. Her bright red headscarf was tied securely around her head. A short man wearing a big straw hat and a blue long-sleeve shirt was behind her. They picked rapidly and moved down the long rows that seemed endless.

Cal quickly pulled cotton from the plants and stuffed them in his bag.

"We can get at least $1.50 for a bag. We'll have enough for a movie and popcorn and much more. Let's hurry. The more we pick, the more money we get," Cal said.

I sweated and coughed from the dust. Cal stopped and offered me a drink of water from the jug.

It was noon.

I felt like I was standing by a bonfire. I sat down on the big chunks of red dirt. We ate our sausage and biscuits in a shadeless row of the cotton field.

Cal frowned. "Your hair is matted from sweat and your face is red," he said.

"So is yours," I snapped.

Cal smiled and lifted me up. "You can ride on the top of my bag."

I jumped on top of the soft, half-full bag. He pulled slowly, a little at a time, filling his bag with cotton. I heard other workers laughing and talking as they filled their bags. Soon Cal's bag felt like a fluffy mattress.

Cal pointed to a wooden wagon.

"See that wagon over there. Let's take the bag and let someone weigh it."

He dragged the stuffed bag over to the scales.

"You have almost 100 pounds, boy," the hired hand informed. "You'll have earned $1.50."

Cal bit his lips and turned away.

"I need more money. I'm going back," he said.

The man shook his head.

"It's too hot for you two to go back. You can empty your bag over there," he said.

Cal took a deep breath, ran his hands through his hair, and emptied the bags. I followed him back to the eternity of white fluff. I wandered in the field far behind him looking for anything but cotton.

Cal waited for me to catch up.

"Stay with me and keep an eye out for snakes," he said.

I scanned the rows this time, not going far away from Cal. I cautiously looked under the bushes and picked small bits of fluff for Cal. I could almost see at any second a snake stretched out across the field.

After what seemed like an eternity, Cal motioned to me. I grabbed my cotton bag, mixed it with his, and headed back to the wagon.

At midafternoon I wanted to go home. I pulled on the back of his sleeveless denim shirt.

"Is it time to go home now?" I asked.

Cal took his handkerchief and wiped my face and hands and tried to get the red dirt off my dress. "Just a few more minutes," he said.

The man weighed his bag—105 pounds. Cal grabbed the sides of his head and squealed.

"Wow, this is amazing," he said.

He held out his hand for the $1.50 and stuffed it in his jeans pocket.

"We did it. Let's go now," he said.

I lumbered behind Cal, slowing him down. My legs hurt, and my stomach fluttered from the heat.

Sunburned and thirsty, we trudged down the dusty road. The house seemed a million miles away.

Cal shouted to Mama, who was waiting on the wooden porch.

"I have $3."

Mama held out her hand.

"Oh good. Thanks, Cal. I need half of that," she said.

Cal gently pulled the money out of his pocket. "Sure, Mama."

Chapter 19

EASTER DAY

I WAS ANXIOUS AND WANTED TO GET AN EARLY START TO MY drive. Easter day had arrived. I had hoped to take Cal for a ride, away from the smell and chaos of the nursing home, but I hadn't been able to find someone to help lift him into the car. Nurse Carol promised to have him ready.

The traffic was scarce. I wondered if everyone had been sleeping in. I pulled into the perfectly planned parking lot. The beautiful brick building posed as a front for elder "non-care."

I entered. I felt like I was stepping into a nameless void containing stale air.

Nurse Carol was buried again in the stacks of charts for her 75 patients. I knew she'd been there all night and had done more than was asked, but she smiled. "Happy Easter," she said.

"I know your family is waiting to celebrate Easter with you. Can you leave soon?" I asked.

She looked up wearily. "I can if the next scheduled nurse comes."

I wanted to say something to help her feel better, but all I could think of to say was, "Thank you for your help."

She smiled and submerged herself again among the stacks.

The halls were busier today, and there was less smell, of course, because it was Easter. If only the visiting families knew.

Mr. Jones, Cal's roommate, was sitting in his wheelchair staring out the glass exit door. He was dressed in his Western shirt, jeans, and house shoes. At least they had changed him into clean clothes. His clothing was different from yesterday.

I stopped to talk.

"Hi, Mr. Jones. Are you going out for Easter?" I asked.

He looked up at me and frowned.

"I'm going to roll my wheelchair to my ranch in that direction," he said. He pointed out the glass door.

I looked out.

"I want to check on my cows," he said.

He was usually a very rational man. He must really want to go home.

I knew he couldn't get the door open.

"That's a long way. I'm sure everything is OK there.

Are you hungry? There's lots of delicious food for Easter in the cafeteria," I said.

I hoped that was true.

He nodded.

I felt heartbroken that no one was there for him. To avoid the painful subject, I moved toward Cal's room to escape the sadness.

"Happy Easter. Cal and I will see you later," I said.

He rubbed his eyes and gestured a slight wave, continuing to stare out the glass door.

Cal was ready and waiting for me. He was wearing a red Texas Ranger baseball T-shirt, loose-fitting sweatpants, and house shoes. I wondered who'd dressed him today. At least he was clean.

"Happy Easter," I said. "I can't get anyone to lift you into the car. Wish we could ride around the countryside when we finish lunch."

Cal looked up. "That's OK. I'm dizzy," he said.

"We can sit outside in the shade in the front and check out the hill in the back. Even if we can't ride somewhere, we will do something interesting.

He acknowledged me with a nod.

I told Nurse Carol that Cal didn't feel well. She found Cal's chart in her stack and checked his meds and then checked his blood pressure. She told me he was OK.

After his lunch, he told me again, "Don't feel good."

Nurse Carol checked him again and found nothing wrong. "Maybe he is coming down with the virus that's going around here. Fresh air will do him good," she said.

A virus going around was not what I wanted to hear.

I pushed him outside into the warm spring air. I found a bench, and we sat outside under the front awning. The lush pink rosebushes were in full bloom. Bugs filled the ground cover that crowded the front flower beds. Cal waved to familiar visitors as they went in the front door.

"Ready to go up the dusty hill out back?" I asked.

He turned and looked at the hill and then back at me.

I eyed the hill. Had I really evaluated the height? The road wound around the hill, which was in my favor. I hoped I could do it.

"We've been around the same sidewalk at the facility so many times. Let's try this. Do you think we can do it?" I asked.

Cal let the comment hang for a few minutes and then pointed to the hill.

I hung my small purse on my shoulder, put a baseball cap on Cal's head, and a bottled water in the pouch of the wheelchair.

"I have my cell phone. We can always call someone to get us," I said.

He leaned forward.

I gripped the handles tightly and started pushing Cal up the hill. The paved, winding road had only been used for dump trucks. The journey up the hill was like trying to climb Mt. Everest. *Maybe I'm far too old for this,* I thought. Feelings of adventure mixed with fear overtook me.

I kept pushing.

My legs ached.

My arms didn't feel like part of my body anymore.

I was sweating.

I was thirsty.

Should I call for help?

I knew 9-1-1 was for emergencies only. The aides couldn't come help us and leave the others. Relatives weren't close enough to come.

What had I done?

I spotted a patch of grass by the winding dirt road. I pushed the wheelchair into the grass and locked the wheels and slowly released myself to the ground. I grabbed the bottled water on my way down.

I opened the water and handed it up to Cal.

We rested another ten minutes. Cal finished his water as if he were refreshing on the Ritz patio looking out at the ocean. I slowly regained my composure.

I think he trusted me, and we were so close to the top. I was determined to keep going. I knew I could do it.

I unlocked the wheels, stretched my stiff legs, and pushed him back on the road. I knew the top was only yards away, but it seemed miles—reachless.

Approaching the top, I felt as if we had just ascended into a lost paradise.

"Wow, we made it to the top. I think only by the grace of God did this happen," I said.

Cal tipped his cap.

I locked the wheels and sat breathless on the ground again beside his wheelchair. We gazed at the crystal blue sky. A curious rabbit darted by. An annoying bee circled overhead. Bluebonnets waved in the breeze, and sweet smells emerged from them. Cal gazed down around him.

The nursing home below seemed like a mirage in the empty landscape. Emerging up over the horizon were cars and trucks heading for the small sleepy town.

He hardly spoke much anymore. He seemed content to sit comfortably now as if he were in a palace garden. The world seemed to open around us. I didn't want to speak for fear the peaceful moments would be lost. I remembered how he used to look, and now the illness had taken its toll. Thirty minutes passed, which seemed like only seconds. I sensed he was getting restless. He twisted in the chair.

"Do you want to go now?"

Cal nodded. "Coffee."

The return was much easier.

I rolled him slowly down the hill, hoping we wouldn't meet an unsuspecting rattlesnake or skunk. I gripped the handles tightly and stopped again in grassy patches to rest. The breeze was cool and seemed to float down with us. We arrived back unscathed.

I left him under the awning out front while I got his coffee.

He lifted his cap and smoothed his thinning hair.

He waved to his friends once more and sipped his beloved coffee.

Once inside again, we looked at the distasteful Easter dinner of dry ham, canned fruit, and a hard-crusted roll. Who was cooking? The food should be special on Easter. Maybe the cook didn't show up for work. I rumbled in my tote, finding the snacks of avocado, spiced apples, and cheddar cheese, glad I had put them in before I left home.

We survived the meal.

"Are you ready to lie down? Do you feel better now?" I asked.

Cal gestured. He seemed to be ready to go back.

When we returned, Mr. Jones was getting a shot so he wouldn't scream anymore.

Sadness filled the room.

Tears wanted to come, but I'd learned in my childhood how to push them down inside.

I knew Cal would wait much longer today for an aide. I pushed the call light early.

An aide showed up an hour later, changed Cal, and lifted him into bed. I fluffed his pillow.

"Good night. I love you," I said.

Cal waved, acknowledging me as he put his head on the pillow.

I took my time strolling to my car, admiring the stunning sunset. What a gift this Easter had been, just enjoying the little things in life and my brother's company.

Cal died the next day.

Chapter 20

TIME

I ONLY WANTED A LITTLE MORE TIME WITH CAL, EVEN THOUGH I had known death was inevitable.

Out of my grief, heartbreak, and confusion, I kept hoping he was OK, as though I could really do something about it now.

I lay awake, staring at the ceiling, feeling helpless. I asked God to somehow let me know that Cal was okay. I closed my eyes hoping to be able to sleep through the night.

I began to dream.

I'm driving once again to the nursing home. I'm listening to my favorite radio station as usual. My car is humming perfectly. There are no other cars on the highway. The sky is bright blue, and the temperature is soothingly cool. I roll down the windows and enjoy the cool breeze on my face.

Suddenly, appearing in the passenger seat is my brother. He looks young again. His bright red hair flows in the wind, and his blue eyes sparkle. He is wearing jeans, his favorite blue shirt, and new work boots. He has a big smile.

"I'm OK," he reassures me.

As suddenly as he appeared, he transformed into a graceful exotic butterfly and soared away, disappearing into the crystal blue sky. I watched in admiration.

I woke up at peace.

Chapter 21
OCEAN

CAL, I WISH YOU WERE HERE WITH ME TO SEE THE powerful ocean. Maybe you are and can come whenever you want. This immaculate beach stretches for miles and is so not like our dry, hot Texas home.

I'm here with you. Can you smell the salty cool air? Can you hear the powerful waves as they lap against the sand? They seem to be wanting to grab our troubles and take them out to sea.

Fearless surfers are weaving through the powerful waves now. They look safe.

The sun peeks through the thick marine layer to give me assurance I'm anchored. The thick fog is like a blanket hovering all around me. However, I can still see surfers, the beach patrol truck, and the flag flying on the guard house. The sight of them calms my reluctance about the approaching fog. The surfers seem to embrace it.

It is not yet spring, and beachcombers are rare, yet there is unexpected activity.

Loud chirps come from birds in the lush trees behind me. Soft, quiet bird sounds are coming from the sandy beach. They sound like nature in concert. Some shorebirds stand quiet and motionless to see what I'm going to do next.

More strong surfers arrive in their wetsuits carrying their sacred boards. More shorebirds swirl into shore, making tracks in the wet sand. I have plenty of company on this quiet beach.

The fog puffs like smoke moistening my paper. Now my hair and clothes are damp. A few sprinkles arrive from the dark, swirling sky. My view of the surfers is getting dimmer. Time to go home now. Maybe next time I'll have more confidence about waves and marine layers.

My visit with Cal and the ocean has been spiritual and mystical. I will take Cal and the ocean with me in my heart.